Messy Bun Hats, *PLUS!*

Pretty and practical, the 10 designs in this headgear collection are a fashion diva's dream. These easy-to-crochet messy bun hats, headwraps, and roomy slouch hats all offer style and comfort that accommodate today's trendy hairdos.

LEISURE ARTS, INC. • Maumelle, Arkansas

Lacy Bun Hat

EASY

Finished Size: Fits 20-22" (51-56 cm) head circumference

SHOPPING LIST

Yarn (Medium Weight) MEDIUM 4

[5 ounces, 256 yards

(141 grams, 234 meters) per skein]:

☐ 1 skein

Crochet Hook

☐ Size I (5.5 mm)

or size needed for gauge

GAUGE INFORMATION

In pattern,

14 sts and Rnds 1-13 = 4" (10 cm)

Gauge Swatch: 4" (10 cm)

Ch 15.

Row 1: Sc in second ch from hook and in each ch across: 14 sc.

Rows 2-14: Ch 1, turn; sc in each sc across.

Finish off.

HAT

Ch 16; join with slip st to form a ring.

Rnd 1 (Right side)**:** Ch 1, work 16 sc in ring; join with slip st to first sc.

Rnd 2: Ch 1, sc in same st as joining, 2 sc in next sc, (sc in next sc, 2 sc in next sc) around; join with slip st to first sc: 24 sc.

Rnd 3: Ch 1, sc in same st as joining and in next sc, 2 sc in next sc, (sc in next 2 sc, 2 sc in next sc) around; join with slip st to first sc: 32 sc.

Rnd 4: Ch 1, sc in same st as joining and in next 2 sc, 2 sc in next sc, (sc in next 3 sc, 2 sc in next sc) around; join with slip st to first sc: 40 sc.

Rnd 5: Ch 1, sc in same st as joining and in next 3 sc, 2 sc in next sc, (sc in next 4 sc, 2 sc in next sc) around; join with slip st to first sc: 48 sc.

Rnd 6: Ch 1, sc in same st as joining and in next 4 sc, 2 sc in next sc, (sc in next 5 sc, 2 sc in next sc) around; join with slip st to first sc: 56 sc.

Rnd 7: Ch 1, sc in same st as joining and in next 5 sc, 2 sc in next sc, (sc in next 6 sc, 2 sc in next sc) around; join with slip st to first sc: 64 sc.

Rnd 8: Ch 3 **(counts as first dc, now and throughout)**, dc **around** first dc ***(Fig. A)***, skip next sc, ★ dc in next sc, dc **around** dc just made, skip next sc; repeat from ★ around; join with slip st to first dc.

Fig. A

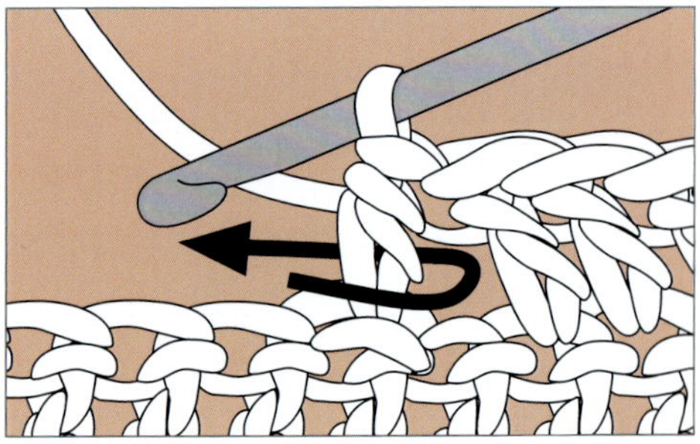

Rnds 9 and 10: Ch 1, sc in same st as joining and in each st around; join with slip st to first sc.

Rnds 11-20: Repeat Rnds 8-10, 3 times; then repeat Row 8 once **more**.

Rnds 21-24: Ch 1, sc in same st as joining and in each st around; join with slip st to first sc.

Finish off.

Wide Headwrap

EASY

Finished Size: Fits 20-22" (51-56 cm) head circumference

SHOPPING LIST

Yarn (Medium Weight) MEDIUM 4

[3.5 ounces, 170 yards (100 grams, 156 meters) per skein]:

- ☐ 1 skein

Crochet Hook

- ☐ Size H (5 mm) **or** size needed for gauge

Additional Supplies

- ☐ Yarn needle

GAUGE INFORMATION

12 hdc = 4" (10 cm);
Rnds 3-7 = 3" (7.5 cm)

Gauge Swatch: 4" (10 cm) square

Ch 13.

Row 1: Hdc in back ridge of second ch from hook and each ch across *(Fig. 1, page 30)*: 12 hdc.

Rows 2-16: Ch 1, turn; working in horizontal bar of each hdc *(Fig. A)*, hdc in first hdc and in each hdc across.

Finish off.

STITCH GUIDE

PUFF STITCH *(abbreviated Puff St)* (uses one st or sp)

★ YO, insert hook in st or sp indicated, YO and pull up a loop even with loop on hook; repeat from ★ 3 times **more**, YO and draw through all 9 loops on hook.

HEADWRAP

Ch 58.

Rnd 1 (Right side)**:** Working in back ridges of beginning ch *(Fig. 1, page 30)*, hdc in second ch from hook and each ch across; being careful **not** to twist piece, join with slip st to first hdc: 57 hdc.

Rnd 2: Ch 2 **(does not count as a st, now and throughout)**, working in horizontal bar of each hdc *(Fig. A)*, hdc in first hdc and in each hdc around; join with slip st to first hdc.

Fig. A

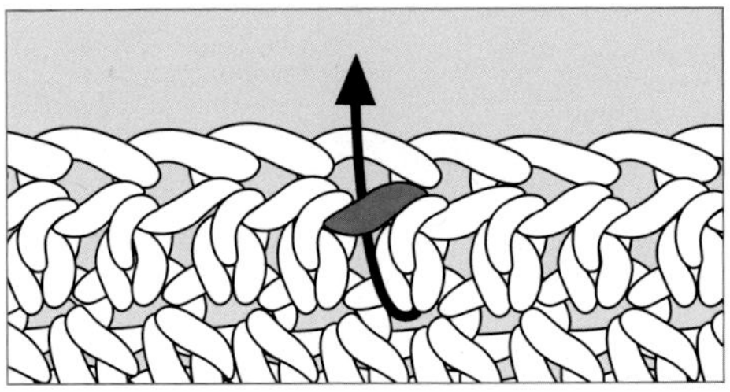

Rnd 3: Ch 2, skip first hdc, work (Puff St, ch 1, Puff St) in next hdc, ★ skip next 2 hdc, work (Puff St, ch 1, Puff St) in next hdc; repeat from ★ around to last hdc, skip last hdc; join with slip st to first Puff St: 38 Puff Sts and 19 ch-1 sps.

Rnd 4: Ch 2, (dc, ch 1, dc) in next ch-1 sp and in each ch-1 sp around; join with slip st to first dc.

Rnd 5: Ch 2, work (Puff St, ch 1, Puff St) in next ch-1 sp and in each ch-1 sp around; join with slip st to first Puff St.

Rnds 6 and 7: Repeat Rnds 4 and 5.

Rnd 8: Ch 2, hdc in first Puff St and in each ch and each Puff St around; join with slip st to first hdc: 57 hdc.

Rnd 9: Ch 2, working in horizontal bar of each hdc, hdc in first hdc and in each hdc around; join with slip st to first hdc, finish off.

Thread yarn needle with beginning end and sew through chs at base of first and last hdc; secure end.

Slouchy Hat

EASY

Finished Size: Fits 20-22" (51-56 cm) head circumference

SHOPPING LIST

Yarn (Medium Weight) 4

[3.5 ounces, 180 yards

(100 grams, 165 meters) per skein]:

☐ 1 skein

Crochet Hook

☐ Size I (5.5 mm)

or size needed for gauge

Additional Supplies

☐ Yarn needle

GAUGE INFORMATION

In pattern,

14 sts and 14 rows/rnds = 4" (10 cm)

Gauge Swatch: 4" (10 cm) square

Ch 15.

Row 1: Working in back ridges of beginning ch *(Fig. 1, page 30)*, sc in second ch from hook, ch 1, (skip next ch, sc in next ch, ch 1) across to last 3 chs, skip next ch, sc in last 2 chs: 14 sts.

Rows 2-14: Ch 1, turn; sc in first sc, (ch 1, sc in next ch-1 sp) across to last sc, sc in last sc.

Finish off.

STITCH GUIDE

FRONT POST DOUBLE CROCHET *(abbreviated FPdc)*

YO, insert hook from **front** to **back** around post of st indicated *(Fig. 4, page 30)*, YO and pull up a loop (3 loops on hook), (YO and draw through 2 loops on hook) twice.

BACK POST DOUBLE CROCHET *(abbreviated BPdc)*

YO, insert hook from **back** to **front** around post of st indicated *(Fig. 4, page 30)*, YO and pull up a loop (3 loops on hook), (YO and draw through 2 loops on hook) twice.

HAT

Ch 61.

Rnd 1 (Right side)**:** Working in back ridges of beginning ch *(Fig. 1, page 30)*, sc in second ch from hook and each ch across; being careful **not** to twist piece, join with slip st to first sc: 60 sc.

Rnds 2-4: Ch 2 **(does not count as a st)**, work FPdc around first 2 sts, work BPdc around next 2 sts, ★ work FPdc around next 2 sts, work BPdc around next 2 sts; repeat from ★ around; join with slip st to Back Loop Only of first FPdc *(Fig. 2, page 30)*.

Rnd 5: Ch 1, working in Back Loops Only, 2 sc in same st as joining, sc in each st around; join with slip st to **both** loops of first sc: 61 sc.

Rnd 6: Ch 1, sc in same st as joining, ★ ch 1, skip next sc, sc in next sc; repeat from ★ around, do **not** join, place marker to indicate beginning of rnd *(see Markers, page 30)*.

Rnds 7-33: (Ch 1, sc in next ch-1 sp) around; at end of Rnd 33, slip st in next sc, finish off leaving a long end for sewing.

Turn piece **wrong** side out and sew top of Hat closed *(see Closing Top of Hat, page 31)*.

Thread yarn needle with beginning end and sew through chs at base of first and last sc; secure end.

Cluster Bun Hat

EASY

Finished Size: Fits 20-22" (51-56 cm) head circumference

SHOPPING LIST

Yarn (Medium Weight) 4

[5 ounces, 256 yards (141 grams, 234 meters) per skein]:

☐ 1 skein

Crochet Hook

☐ Size I (5.5 mm) **or** size needed for gauge

Additional Supplies

☐ Yarn needle

GAUGE INFORMATION

In pattern,

(Cluster, ch 1) 6 times and 7 rnds = 4" (10 cm);

Gauge Swatch: 4" (10 cm) square

Ch 13.

Row 1: Working in back ridges of beginning ch ***(Fig. 1, page 30)***, sc in second ch from hook and in each ch across: 12 sc.

Rows 2-12: Ch 1, turn; sc in each sc across.

Finish off.

STITCH GUIDE

CLUSTER (uses one st or sp)

★ YO, insert hook in st or sp indicated, YO and pull up a loop, YO and draw through 2 loops on hook; repeat from ★ 2 times **more**, YO and draw through all 4 loops on hook.

SINGLE CROCHET 2 TOGETHER ***(abbreviated sc2tog)***

Pull up a loop in each of next 2 sts, YO and draw through all 3 loops on hook **(counts as one sc)**.

HAT

Ch 65.

Rnd 1 (Right side)**:** Working in back ridges of beginning ch ***(Fig. 1, page 30)***, sc in second ch from hook and each ch across; being careful **not** to twist piece, join with slip st to first sc: 64 sc.

Rnds 2-5: Ch 1, sc in each sc around; join with slip st to first sc.

Rnd 6: Ch 2 **(does not count as a st, now and throughout)**, work Cluster in same st as joining, ch 1, skip next sc, ★ work Cluster in next sc, ch 1, skip next sc; repeat from ★ around; join with slip st to top of first Cluster: 32 Clusters and 32 ch-1 sps.

Rnds 7-13: Slip st in next ch-1 sp, ch 2, work Cluster in same sp, ch 1, (work Cluster in next ch-1 sp, ch 1) around; join with slip st to top of first Cluster.

Rnd 14: Ch 1, sc in same st as joining and in next 5 sts, sc2tog, (sc in next 6 sts, sc2tog) around; join with slip st to first sc: 56 sc.

Rnd 15: Ch 1, sc in same st as joining and in next 4 sc, sc2tog, (sc in next 5 sc, sc2tog) around; join with slip st to first sc: 48 sc.

Rnd 16: Ch 1, sc in same st as joining and in next 3 sc, sc2tog, (sc in next 4 sc, sc2tog) around; join with slip st to first sc: 40 sc.

Rnd 17: Ch 1, sc in same st as joining and in next 2 sc, sc2tog, (sc in next 3 sc, sc2tog) around; join with slip st to first sc: 32 sc.

Rnd 18: Ch 1, sc in same st as joining and in next sc, sc2tog, (sc in next 2 sc, sc2tog) around; join with slip st to first sc: 24 sc.

Rnd 19: Ch 1, sc in same st as joining, sc2tog, (sc in next sc, sc2tog) around; join with slip st to first sc, finish off.

Thread yarn needle with beginning end and sew through chs at base of first and last sc; secure end.

Ribbed Bun Hat

Shown on pages 12 and 13.

EASY

Finished Size: Fits 20-22" (51-56 cm) head circumference

SHOPPING LIST

Yarn (Medium Weight) MEDIUM 4

[5 ounces, 256 yards

(141 grams, 234 meters) per skein]:

☐ 1 skein

Crochet Hook

☐ Size G (4 mm)

or size needed for gauge

GAUGE INFORMATION

In pattern,

16 sts and 16 rows/rnds = 4" (10 cm)

Gauge Swatch: 4" (10 cm) square

Ch 17.

Row 1: Sc in second ch from hook and in each ch across: 16 sc.

Rows 2-16: Ch 1, turn; sc in each sc across.

Finish off.

STITCH GUIDE

BACK POST SINGLE CROCHET *(abbreviated BPsc)*

Insert hook from **back** to **front** around post of st indicated ***(Fig. 4, page 30)***, YO and pull up a loop, YO and draw through both loops on hook.

FRONT POST DOUBLE CROCHET *(abbreviated FPdc)*

YO, insert hook from **front** to **back** around post of st indicated ***(Fig. 4, page 30)***, YO and pull up a loop (3 loops on hook), (YO and draw through 2 loops on hook) twice.

HAT

Ch 18; join with slip st to form a ring.

Rnd 1 (Right side)**:** Ch 1, work 18 sc in ring; join with slip st to first sc.

Rnd 2: Ch 2 **(does not count as a st, now and throughout)**, work FPdc around same st as joining, 2 sc in next sc, (work FPdc around next sc, 2 sc in next sc) around; join with slip st to first FPdc: 27 sts.

Rnd 3: Ch 2, work FPdc around same st as joining, sc in next sc, 2 sc in next sc, ★ work FPdc around next FPdc, sc in next sc, 2 sc in next sc; repeat from ★ around; join with slip st to first FPdc: 36 sts.

Rnd 4: Ch 2, work FPdc around same st as joining, sc in next 2 sc, 2 sc in next sc, ★ work FPdc around next FPdc, sc in next 2 sc, 2 sc in next sc; repeat from ★ around; join with slip st to first FPdc: 45 sts.

Rnd 5: Ch 2, work FPdc around same st as joining, sc in next 3 sc, 2 sc in next sc, ★ work FPdc around next FPdc, sc in next 3 sc, 2 sc in next sc; repeat from ★ around; join with slip st to first FPdc: 54 sts.

Rnd 6: Ch 2, work FPdc around same st as joining, sc in next 4 sc, 2 sc in next sc, ★ work FPdc around next FPdc, sc in next 4 sc, 2 sc in next sc; repeat from ★ around; join with slip st to first FPdc: 63 sts.

Rnd 7: Ch 2, work FPdc around same st as joining, sc in next 5 sc, 2 sc in next sc, ★ work FPdc around next FPdc, sc in next 5 sc, 2 sc in next sc; repeat from ★ around; join with slip st to first FPdc: 72 sts.

Rnds 8-15: Ch 2, work FPdc around same st as joining, sc in next 7 sc, (work FPdc around next FPdc, sc in next 7 sc) around; join with slip st to first FPdc.

Rnds 16-19: Ch 2, work FPdc around same st as joining, sc in next 3 sc, (work FPdc around next st, sc in next 3 sc) around; join with slip st to first FPdc.

Rnds 20-24: Ch 2, work FPdc around same st as joining, sc in next sc, (work FPdc around next st, sc in next sc) around; join with slip st to first FPdc.

Rnds 25-27: Ch 2, work FPdc around same st as joining and each st around; join with slip st to first FPdc.

Rnd 28: Ch 1, work BPsc around same st as joining and each FPdc around; join with slip st to first BPsc, finish off.

Floral Headwrap

EASY

Finished Size: Fits 20-22" (51-56 cm) head circumference

SHOPPING LIST

Yarn (Medium Weight) 4

[3.5 ounces, 170 yards

(100 grams, 156 meters) per skein]:

☐ 1 skein

Crochet Hook

☐ Size I (5.5 mm)

or size needed for gauge

Additional Supplies

☐ 1 1/8" (29 mm) button - 2

☐ Sewing needle and thread

GAUGE INFORMATION

In pattern, 12 sts = 4" (10 cm);

5 rows = 3¼" (8.25 cm)

Gauge Swatch: 4" wide x 3¼" high (10 cm x 8.25 cm)

Ch 15.

Row 1: Tr in fifth ch from hook **(4 skipped chs count as first tr)** and in each ch across: 12 tr.

Rows 2-4: Ch 3 **(counts as first dc)**, turn; dc in next st and in each st across.

Row 5: Ch 4, turn; tr in next dc and in each dc across; finish off.

STITCH GUIDE

TREBLE CROCHET *(abbreviated tr)*

YO twice, insert hook in st indicated, YO and pull up a loop (4 loops on hook), (YO and draw through 2 loops on hook) 3 times.

HEADWRAP

Ch 67.

Row 1 (Right side)**:** Sc in second ch from hook and in next 5 chs, hdc in next 4 chs, dc in next 4 chs, tr in next 38 chs, dc in next 4 chs, hdc in next 4 chs, sc in last 6 chs: 66 sts.

Note: Loop a short piece of yarn around any stitch to mark Row 1 as **right** side.

Row 2: Ch 1, turn; slip st in first 6 sc, sc in next 4 hdc, hdc in next 4 dc, dc in next 38 tr, hdc in next 4 dc, sc in next 4 hdc, slip st in last 6 sc.

Row 3: Ch 1, turn; slip st in first 6 slip sts, sc in next 4 sc, hdc in next 4 hdc, dc in next 38 dc, hdc in next 4 hdc, sc in next 4 sc, slip st in next 2 slip sts, [ch 2, skip next 2 slip sts **(buttonhole made)**], slip st in last 2 slip sts: 64 sts and one ch-2 sp.

Row 4: Ch 1, turn; slip st in first 2 slip sts and in next 2 chs, slip st in next 2 slip sts, sc in next 4 sc, hdc in next 4 hdc, dc in next 38 dc, hdc in next 4 hdc, sc in next 4 sc, slip st in last 6 slip sts: 66 sts.

Row 5: Ch 1, turn, sc in first 6 slip sts, hdc in next 4 sc, dc in next 4 hdc, tr in next 38 dc, dc in next 4 hdc, hdc in next 4 sc, sc in last 6 slip sts; do **not** finish off.

Edging: Ch 1, do **not** turn; working from **left** to **right**, work reverse sc ***(Figs. 5a-d, page 30)*** in each st across; work reverse sc in end of each row across; working in free loops of beginning ch ***(Fig. 3, page 30)***, work reverse sc in each ch across; work reverse sc in end of each row across; join with slip st to first st, finish off.

FLOWER

Ch 5; join with slip st to form a ring.

Rnd 1 (Right side)**:** (Ch 4, slip st in ring) 6 times: 6 ch-4 sps.

Rnd 2: Slip st in first ch-4 sp, (ch 1, 4 dc in same sp) twice, ★ slip st in next ch-4 sp, (ch 1, 4 dc in same sp) twice; repeat from ★ around; join with slip st to first slip st, finish off.

With **right** side facing, sew one button to end of Headwrap opposite buttonhole.

Using photo on page 15 as a guide for placement, sew remaining button to Row 3. To attach Flower, slip beginning ring over button.

Two-Tone Bun Hat

Shown on page 18.

EASY

Finished Size: Fits 20-22" (51-56 cm) head circumference

SHOPPING LIST

Yarn (Medium Weight) MEDIUM 4

[4 ounces, 203 yards (113 grams, 186 meters) per skein]:

- ☐ Pink - 1 skein
- ☐ Cream - 1 skein

Crochet Hooks

- ☐ Size G (4 mm) **and**
- ☐ Size H (5 mm)

or sizes needed for gauge

Additional Supplies

- ☐ Yarn needle
- ☐ Sewing needle and thread
- ☐ 1½" (38 mm) button

GAUGE INFORMATION

With larger size hook,
in Brim pattern, 12 sts = 4" (10 cm)
With smaller size hook,
16 sc and 16 rows/rnds = 4" (10 cm)

Gauge Swatch: 4" (10 cm) square

With smaller size hook and Cream, ch 17.

Row 1: Working in back ridges of beginning ch ***(Fig. 1, page 30)***, sc in second ch from hook and in each ch across: 16 sc.

Rows 2-16: Ch 1, turn; sc in each sc across.

Finish off.

STITCH GUIDE

FRONT POST TREBLE CROCHET ***(abbreviated FPtr)***

YO twice, insert hook from **front** to **back** around post of st indicated ***(Fig. 4, page 30)***, YO and pull up a loop (4 loops on hook), (YO and draw through 2 loops on hook) 3 times.

SINGLE CROCHET 2 TOGETHER ***(abbreviated sc2tog)***

Pull up a loop in each of next 2 sts, YO and draw through all 3 loops on hook **(counts as one sc)**.

BRIM

With larger size hook and Pink, ch 68.

Row 1: Sc in back ridge of second ch from hook and each ch across ***(Fig. 1, page 30)***, place marker around last sc made for st placement: 67 sc.

Rows 2 and 3: Ch 1, turn; sc in each sc across.

Row 4 (Right side)**:** Ch 1, turn; sc in first 2 sc, work FPtr around marked sc 3 rows **below**, skip next 4 sc, work FPtr around next sc, ★ skip next 2 sc from last sc made, sc in next 4 sc, work FPtr around next sc from last FPtr made, skip next 4 sc, work FPtr around next sc; repeat from ★ across to last 5 sc, skip next 2 sc from last sc made, sc in last 3 sc.

Rows 5-7: Ch 1, turn; sc in each st across.

Row 8: Ch 1, turn; skip first 2 sc 3 rows **below**, work FPtr around next sc, skip first sc on previous row, sc in next 4 sc, work FPtr around next sc from last FPtr made, ★ skip next 4 sc, work FPtr around next sc, skip next 2 sc from last sc made, sc in next 4 sc, work FPtr around next sc from last FPtr made; repeat from ★ across to last 2 sc, skip next sc from last sc made, sc in last sc.

Rows 9-11: Ch 1, turn; sc in each st across.

Row 12: Ch 1, turn; sc in first 2 sc, work FPtr around first sc 3 rows **below**, skip next 4 sc, work FPtr around next sc, ★ skip next 2 sc from last sc made, sc in next 4 sc, work FPtr around next sc from last FPtr made, skip next 4 sc, work FPtr around next sc; repeat from ★ across to last 5 sc, skip next 2 sc from last sc made, sc in last 3 sc; finish off leaving a long end for sewing.

BUTTON TAB

Row 1: With larger size hook and **right** side facing, join Pink with sc in end of Row 4 *(see Joining With Sc, page 30)*; sc in end of next 5 rows, leave remaining rows unworked: 6 sc.

Row 2: Ch 1, turn; sc in each sc across.

Row 3: Ch 1, turn; sc in first 2 sc, [ch 2, skip next 2 sc (**buttonhole made**)], sc in last 2 sc: 4 sc and one ch-2 sp.

Rnd 4: Ch 1, turn; sc in first 2 sc, 2 sc in next ch-2 sp, sc in last 2 sc: 6 sc.

Rnd 5: Ch 1, turn; sc in each sc across; finish off.

Thread yarn needle with long end from Brim. With **wrong** side together, sew ends of rows together, being careful to place Button Tab on **right** side.

BODY

Rnd 1: With **right** side facing, fold Brim with seam at one edge, with smaller size hook, join Cream with sc in st at opposite edge; sc in each st around; join with slip st to first sc: 67 sc.

Rnd 2: Ch 1, sc in each sc around; do **not** join, place marker to indicate beginning of rnd *(see Markers, page 30)*.

Rnds 3-10: Sc in each sc around.

Rnd 11: Sc2tog, sc in each sc around: 66 sc.

Rnd 12: (Sc in next 4 sc, sc2tog) around: 55 sc.

Rnd 13: (Sc in next 3 sc, sc2tog) around: 44 sc.

Rnd 14: (Sc in next 2 sc, sc2tog) around: 33 sc.

Rnd 15: (Sc in next sc, sc2tog) around: 22 sc.

Rnd 16: Sc in next 2 sc, sc2tog, (sc in next sc, sc2tog) 6 times; slip st in next sc, finish off.

Sew button to Brim.

Ribbon Bun Hat

EASY

Finished Size: Fits 20-22" (51-56 cm) head circumference

SHOPPING LIST

Yarn (Medium Weight) 4

[5 ounces, 256 yards (141 grams, 234 meters) per skein]:

☐ 1 skein

Crochet Hook

☐ Size I (5.5 mm)
or size needed for gauge

Additional Supplies

☐ 5/8" (16 mm) wide ribbon - 1 yard (1 meter)

GAUGE INFORMATION

In pattern,
2 repeats (14 sts) = 4¼" (10.75);
6 rows/rnds = 3" (7.5 cm)

Gauge Swatch: 4¼" wide x 3" high (10.75 cm x 7.5 cm)

Ch 16.

Row 1: Dc in fourth ch from hook and in each ch across: 14 sts.

Rows 2-6: Ch 3, turn; dc in next dc and in each st across.

Finish off.

STITCH GUIDE

FRONT POST DOUBLE CROCHET ***(abbreviated FPdc)***

YO, insert hook from **front** to **back** around post of st indicated ***(Fig. 4, page 30)***, YO and pull up a loop (3 loops on hook), (YO and draw through 2 loops on hook) twice.

SINGLE CROCHET 2 TOGETHER ***(abbreviated sc2tog)***

Pull up a loop in each of next 2 sts, YO and draw through all 3 loops on hook **(counts as one sc)**.

BODY

Ch 65, place marker in third ch from hook for st placement.

Rnd 1 (Right side)**:** Dc in fourth ch from hook **(3 skipped chs count as first dc)** and in next ch, ch 2, skip next 2 chs, dc in next 5 chs, ch 2, ★ skip next 2 chs, dc in next 5 chs, ch 2; repeat from ★ across to last 4 chs, skip next 2 chs, dc in last 2 chs; being careful **not** to twist piece, join with slip st to first dc: 45 dc and 9 ch-2 sps.

Note: Loop a short piece of yarn around any stitch to mark Rnd 1 as **right** side.

Rnd 2: Ch 2 **(does not count as a st, now and throughout)**, work FPdc around first dc, skip next 2 dc, 6 dc in next ch-2 sp, skip next 2 dc, ★ work FPdc around next dc, skip next 2 dc, 6 dc in next ch-2 sp, skip next 2 dc; repeat from ★ around; join with slip st to first FPdc: 63 sts.

Rnd 3: Ch 2, work FPdc around first FPdc, dc in next 2 dc, ch 2, skip next 2 dc, dc in next 2 dc, ★ work FPdc around next FPdc, dc in next 2 dc, ch 2, skip next 2 dc, dc in next 2 dc; repeat from ★ around; join with slip st to first FPdc: 45 sts and 9 ch-2 sps.

Rnds 4-11: Repeat Rnds 2 and 3, 4 times.

Rnd 12: Ch 2, work FPdc around first dc, skip next 2 dc, 4 dc in next ch-2 sp, skip next 2 dc, ★ work FPdc around next dc, skip next 2 dc, 4 dc in next ch-2 sp, skip next 2 dc; repeat from ★ around; join with slip st to first FPdc: 45 sts.

Rnd 13: Ch 2, work FPdc around first FPdc, dc in next dc, ch 1, skip next 2 dc, dc in next dc, ★ work FPdc around next FPdc, dc in next dc, ch 1, skip next 2 dc, dc in next dc; repeat from ★ around; join with slip st to first FPdc: 27 sts and 9 ch-1 sps.

Rnd 14: Ch 2, work FPdc around first FPdc, skip next dc, 2 dc in next ch-1 sp, skip next dc, ★ work FPdc around next FPdc, skip next dc, 2 dc in next ch-1 sp, skip next dc; repeat from ★ around; join with slip st to first FPdc: 27 sts.

Rnd 15: Ch 1, sc in same st as joining, sc2tog, (sc in next st, sc2tog) around; join with slip st to first sc, finish off.

BOTTOM EDGING

Rnd 1: With **right** side facing and working in free loops ***(Fig. 3, page 30)*** and in sps across beginning ch, join yarn with sc in marked ch ***(see Joining With Sc, page 30)***; remove marker, sc in next 2 chs, 2 sc in next sp, (sc in next 5 chs, 2 sc in next sp) around to last 2 chs, sc in last 2 chs; join with slip st to first sc: 63 sc.

Rnd 2: Ch 1, sc in same st as joining and in next 4 sc, sc2tog, (sc in next 5 sc, sc2tog) around; join with slip st to first sc: 54 sc.

Rnd 3: Ch 1, sc in same st as joining and in each sc around; join with slip st to first sc, finish off.

Using photo as a guide, weave ribbon through ch-2 sps on Rnd 1 of Body; tie ends in a bow.

Wide Brim Bun Hat

Shown on pages 24 and 25.

EASY

Finished Size: Fits 20-22" (51-56 cm) head circumference

SHOPPING LIST

Yarn (Medium Weight) 4
[3.5 ounces, 270 yards
(100 grams, 247 meters) per skein]:
- ☐ 1 skein

Crochet Hook
- ☐ Size H (5 mm)
  or size needed for gauge

GAUGE INFORMATION

In Brim pattern,
12 hdc and 8 rows = 3" (7.5 cm)
Gauge Swatch: 3" (7.5 cm) square
Work same as Brim through Row 8:
12 hdc.

STITCH GUIDE

HALF DOUBLE CROCHET 2 TOGETHER *(abbreviated hdc2tog)*
★ YO, insert hook in **next** hdc, YO and pull up a loop; repeat from ★ once **more**, YO and draw through all 5 loops on hook **(counts as one hdc)**.

BRIM

Ch 13.

Row 1 (Wrong side)**:** Hdc in second ch from hook and in each ch across: 12 hdc.

Note: Loop a short piece of yarn around back of any stitch on Row 1 to mark **right** side.

Row 2: Ch 1, working in Back Loops Only *(Fig. 2, page 30)*, hdc in first hdc and in each hdc across.

Row 3: Ch 1, turn; working in Front Loops Only *(Fig. 2, page 30)*, hdc in first hdc and in each hdc across.

Rows 4-54: Repeat Rows 2 and 3, 25 times; then repeat Row 2 once **more**; do **not** finish off.

Joining: Ch 1, with **wrong** side together, working in free loops of beginning ch ***(Fig. 3, page 30)* and** in both loops of sts across Row 54, slip st in each st across; do **not** finish off.

BODY

Rnd 1: Ch 1, hdc in end of each row around; join with slip st to first hdc: 54 hdc.

Rnd 2: Ch 1, hdc in each hdc around; do **not** join, place marker to indicate beginning of rnd ***(see Markers, page 30)***.

Rnds 3-9: Hdc in each hdc around.

Rnd 10: (Hdc in next 7 hdc, hdc2tog) around: 48 hdc.

Rnd 11: (Hdc in next 6 hdc, hdc2tog) around: 42 hdc.

Rnd 12: (Hdc in next 5 hdc, hdc2tog) around: 36 hdc.

Rnd 13: (Hdc in next 4 hdc, hdc2tog) around: 30 hdc.

Rnd 14: (Hdc in next 3 hdc, hdc2tog) around: 24 hdc.

Rnd 15: (Hdc in next 2 hdc, hdc2tog) around; slip st in next hdc: 18 hdc.

Rnd 16: Ch 1, working from **left** to **right**, work reverse sc in each hdc around ***(Figs. 5a-d, page 30)***; join with slip st to first st, finish off.

Brim Edging: With **right** side facing, join yarn with slip st in seam; ch 1, hdc in end of each row around; join with slip st to first hdc, finish off.

Cabled Brim Hat

EASY

Finished Size: Fits 20-22" (51-56 cm) head circumference

SHOPPING LIST

Yarn (Medium Weight) MEDIUM 4
[5 ounces, 256 yards
(141 grams, 234 meters) per skein]:
☐ 1 skein

Crochet Hook
☐ Size I (5.5 mm)
or size needed for gauge

Additional Supplies
☐ Yarn needle
☐ Sewing needle and thread
☐ 1½" (38 mm) button

GAUGE INFORMATION

14 sc and 14 rows/rnds = 4" (10 cm)
Gauge Swatch: 4" (10 cm) square
Ch 15.
Row 1: Working in back ridges of beginning ch *(Fig. 1, page 30)*, sc in second ch from hook and in each ch across: 14 sc.
Rows 2-14: Ch 1, turn; sc in each sc across.
Finish off.

STITCH GUIDE

FRONT POST TREBLE CROCHET *(abbreviated FPtr)*
YO twice, insert hook from **front** to **back** around post of st indicated *(Fig. 4, page 30)*, YO and pull up a loop (4 loops on hook), (YO and draw through 2 loops on hook) 3 times.

FRONT POST DOUBLE CROCHET *(abbreviated FPdc)*
YO, insert hook from **front** to **back** around post of st indicated *(Fig. 4, page 30)*, YO and pull up a loop (3 loops on hook), (YO and draw through 2 loops on hook) twice.

BRIM

Ch 65.

Rnd 1 (Right side)**:** Working in back ridges of beginning ch *(Fig. 1, page 30)*, sc in second ch from hook and in each ch across; being careful **not** to twist piece, join with slip st to first sc: 64 sc.

Rnds 2 and 3: Ch 2 **(does not count as a st, now and throughout)**; work FPdc around first st and each st around; join with slip st to first FPdc.

Rnd 4: Ch 2, skip first 2 FPdc, work FPtr around next 2 FPdc, working in **front** of FPtr just made, work FPtr around 2 skipped FPdc, ★ skip next 2 FPdc, work FPtr around next 2 FPdc, working in **front** of FPtr just made, work FPtr around 2 skipped FPdc; repeat from ★ around; join with slip st to first FPtr.

Rnds 5-9: Repeat Rnds 2-4 once, then repeat Rnds 2 and 3 once **more**.

BODY

Rnd 1: Ch 1, sc in each FPdc around; do **not** join, place marker to indicate beginning of rnd ***(see Markers, page 30)***.

Rnds 2-21: Sc in each sc around; at end of Rnd 21, slip st in next sc, finish off leaving a long end for sewing.

Turn piece **wrong** side out and sew top of Hat closed ***(see Closing Top of Hat, page 31)***.

Thread yarn needle with beginning end and sew through chs at base of first and last sc; secure end.

Using photo as a guide for placement, sew button to Rnd 2 of Brim.

General Instructions

ABBREVIATIONS

BPdc	Back Post double crochet(s)
BPsc	Back Post single crochet(s)
ch(s)	chain(s)
cm	centimeters
dc	double crochet(s)
FPdc	Front Post double crochet(s)
FPtr	Front Post treble crochet(s)
hdc	half double crochet(s)
hdc2tog	half double crochet 2 together
mm	millimeters
Rnd(s)	Round(s)
sc	single crochet(s)
sc2tog	single crochet 2 together
sp(s)	space(s)
st(s)	stitch(es)
tr	treble crochet(s)
YO	yarn over

SYMBOLS & TERMS

★ — work instructions following ★ as many **more** times as indicated in addition to the first time.

( ) or **[ ]** — work enclosed instructions **as many** times as specified by the number immediately following **or** work all enclosed instructions in the stitch or space indicated **or** contains explanatory remarks.

colon (:) — the number(s) given after a colon at the end of a row or round denote(s) the number of stitches or spaces you should have on that row or round.

GAUGE

Exact gauge is **essential** for proper size. Before beginning your project, make the sample swatch given in the individual instructions in the yarn and hook specified. After completing the swatch, measure it, counting your stitches and rows carefully. If your swatch is larger or smaller than specified, **make another, changing hook size to get the correct gauge.** Keep trying until you find the size hook that will give you the specified gauge.

CROCHET TERMINOLOGY		
UNITED STATES		INTERNATIONAL
slip stitch (slip st)	=	single crochet (sc)
single crochet (sc)	=	double crochet (dc)
half double crochet (hdc)	=	half treble crochet (htr)
double crochet (dc)	=	treble crochet (tr)
treble crochet (tr)	=	double treble crochet (dtr)
double treble crochet (dtr)	=	triple treble crochet (ttr)
triple treble crochet (tr tr)	=	quadruple treble crochet (qtr)
skip	=	miss

Yarn Weight Symbol & Names	LACE 0	SUPER FINE 1	FINE 2	LIGHT 3	MEDIUM 4	BULKY 5	SUPER BULKY 6	JUMBO 7
Type of Yarns in Category	Fingering, size 10 crochet thread	Sock, Fingering, Baby	Sport, Baby	DK, Light Worsted	Worsted, Afghan, Aran	Chunky, Craft, Rug	Super Bulky, Roving	Jumbo, Roving
Crochet Gauge* Ranges in Single Crochet to 4" (10 cm)	32-42 sts**	21-32 sts	16-20 sts	12-17 sts	11-14 sts	8-11 sts	6-9 sts	5 sts and fewer
Advised Hook Size Range	Steel*** 6 to 8, Regular hook B-1	B-1 to E-4	E-4 to 7	7 to I-9	I-9 to K-10½	K-10½ to M/N-13	M/N-13 to Q	Q and larger

*GUIDELINES ONLY: The chart above reflects the most commonly used gauges and hook sizes for specific yarn categories.

BEGINNER	Projects for first-time crocheters using basic stitches. Minimal shaping.
EASY	Projects using yarn with basic stitches, repetitive stitch patterns, simple color changes, and simple shaping and finishing.
INTERMEDIATE	Projects using a variety of techniques, such as basic lace patterns or color patterns, mid-level shaping and finishing.
EXPERIENCED	Projects with intricate stitch patterns, techniques and dimension, such as non-repeating patterns, multi-color techniques, fine threads, small hooks, detailed shaping and refined finishing.

CROCHET HOOKS																
U.S.	B-1	C-2	D-3	E-4	F-5	G-6	7	H-8	I-9	J-10	K-10½	L-11	M/N-13	N/P-15	P/Q	Q	S
Metric - mm	2.25	2.75	3.25	3.5	3.75	4	4.5	5	5.5	6	6.5	8	9	10	15	16	19

JOINING WITH SC

When instructed to join with sc, begin with a slip knot on hook. Insert hook in stitch or space indicated, YO and pull up a loop, YO and draw through both loops on hook.

MARKERS

Markers are used to help distinguish the beginning of each round being worked. Place a 2" (5 cm) scrap piece of yarn before the first stitch of each round, moving marker after each round is complete.

BACK RIDGE

Work only in loops indicated by arrows *(Fig. 1)*.

Fig. 1

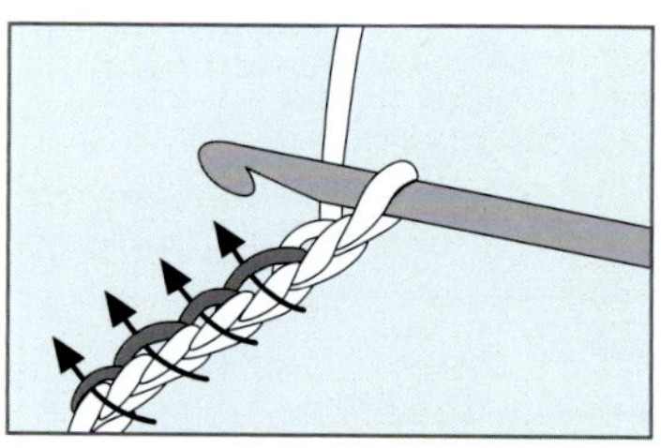

BACK OR FRONT LOOP ONLY

Work only in loop(s) indicated by arrow *(Fig. 2)*.

Fig. 2

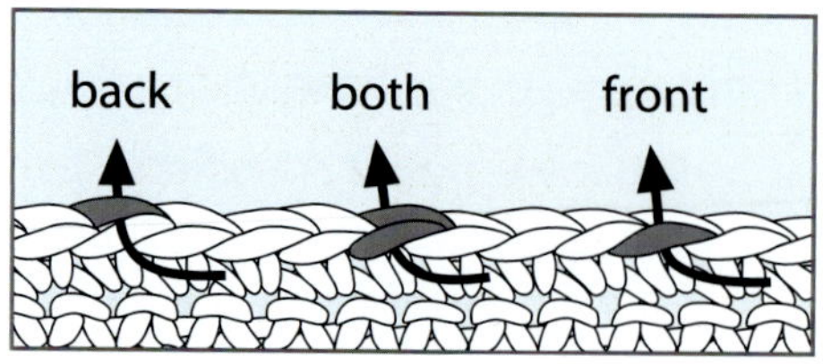

FREE LOOPS OF A CHAIN

When instructed to work in free loops of a chain, work in loop indicated by arrow *(Fig. 3)*.

Fig. 3

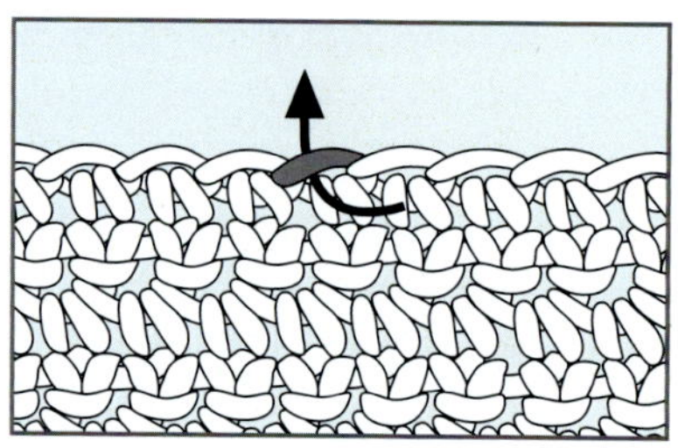

POST STITCH

Work around post of stitch indicated, inserting hook in direction of arrow *(Fig. 4)*.

Fig. 4

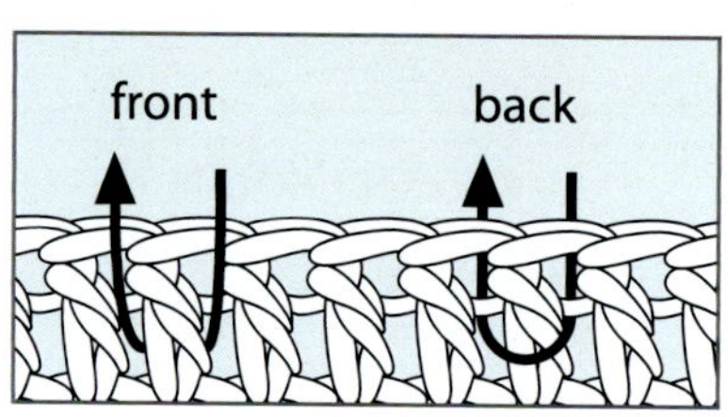

REVERSE SINGLE CROCHET

(abbreviated reverse sc)

Working from **left** to **right**, ★ insert hook in st to right of hook ***(Fig. 5a)***, YO and draw through, under and to left of loop on hook (2 loops on hook) ***(Fig. 5b)***, YO and draw through both loops on hook ***(Fig. 5c)*** **(reverse sc made, *Fig. 5d*)**; repeat from ★ around.

Fig. 5a

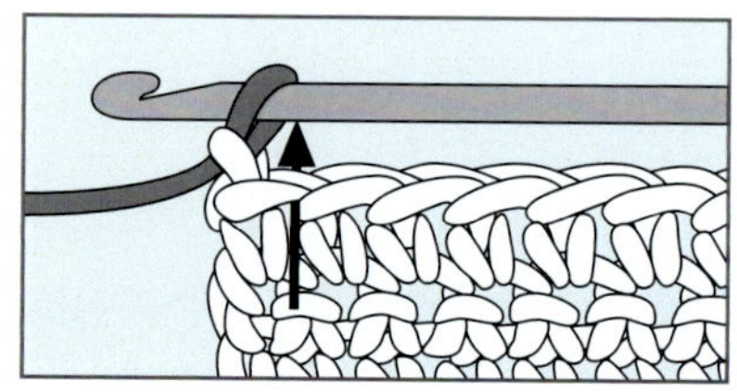

Fig. 5b

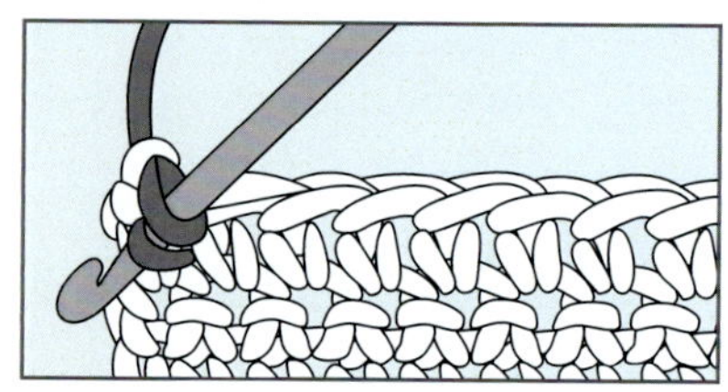

Fig. 5c

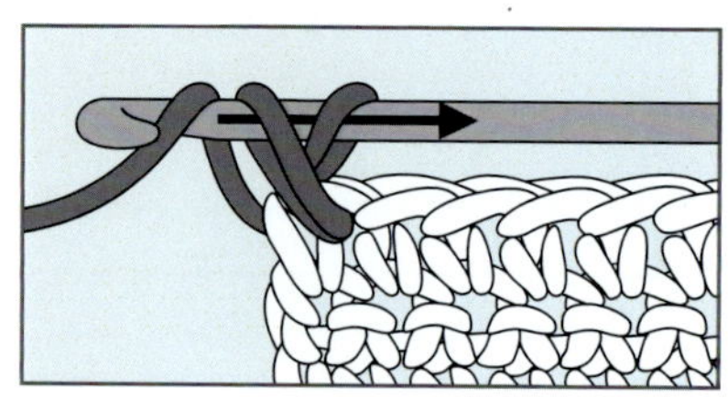

Fig. 5d

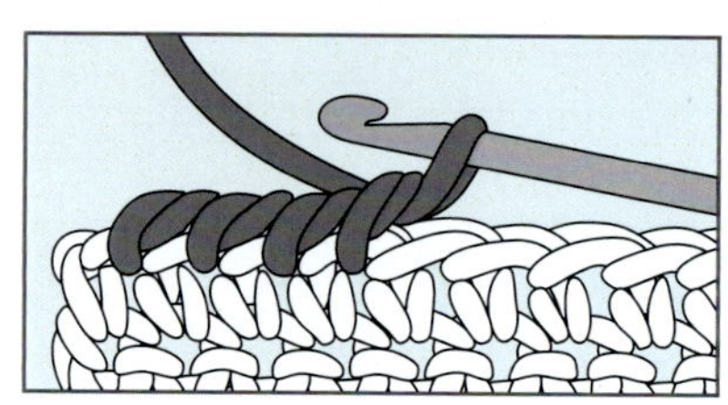

CLOSING TOP OF HAT

Turn piece **wrong** side out. Using scrap pieces of yarn, pins, or split-ring markers, place 8 markers evenly spaced around top of hat, having first marker where long end is attached to piece. Thread yarn needle with long end. Following diagram, sew through fabric at 2, bringing 1 and 2 together at center. Continue sewing through marked areas numerically, having each meet at center; secure end.

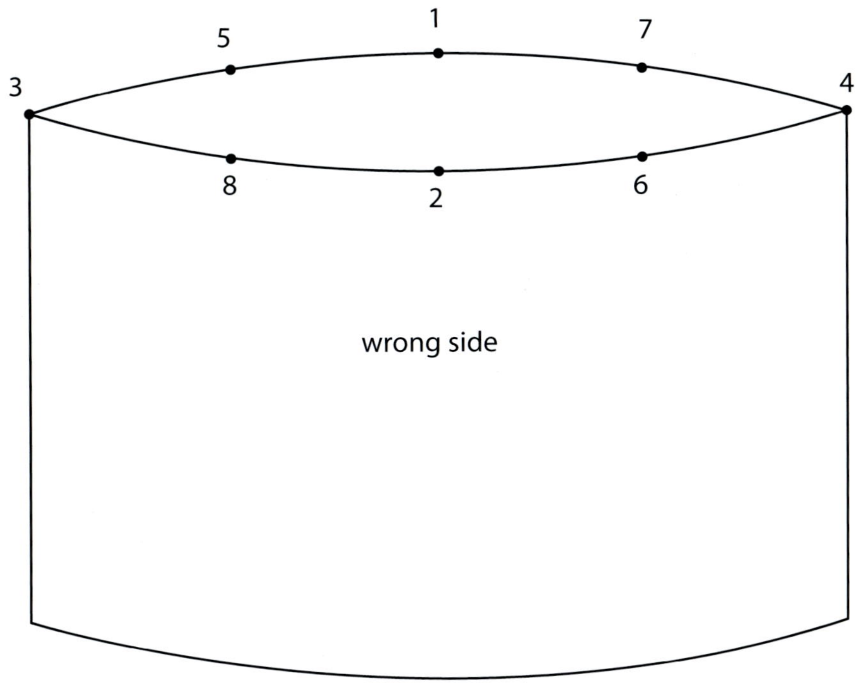

Meet the Designer:

Kristi Simpson

Inspired by her love of yarn, Kristi Simpson creates crochet and knit patterns with a fresh and modern touch. The mother of five became hooked on crochet after teaching herself so she could help her daughter make a scarf from a "learn to crochet" kit that was a gift.

"I loved it from the beginning," she says. "I was amazed that I could take a string of yarn and create something so useful and pretty! Needless to say, I never stopped!"

Other Leisure Arts books featuring Kristi's designs include *Huggable Amigurumi* (#7163), *Color-Block Baby Blankets* (#7104), *Rucksacks and Backpacks* (#7058), *Lacy Wraps* (#6995), *Urban Slouch Hats* (#6796), *Easy Essential Bags* (#6795), *Animal Baby Bibs* (#6850), *Animal Blankets* (#6996), *Sweet and Sporty Diaper Covers* (#6719), and *Modern Baby Booties* (#6914). Visit kristisimpson.net or find her on Ravelry, Facebook, and Pinterest.

Yarn Information

Each item in this book was made using Medium Weight Yarn. Any brand of Medium Weight Yarn may be used. It is best to refer to the yardage/meters when determining how many balls or skeins to purchase. Remember, to arrive at the finished size, it is the GAUGE/TENSION that is important, not the brand of yarn.

For your convenience, listed below are the specific yarns used to create our photography models. Because yarn manufacturers make frequent changes to their product lines, you may sometimes find it necessary to use a substitute yarn or to search for the discontinued product at alternate suppliers (locally or online).

LACY BUN HAT
Red Heart® Soft®
#4608 Wine

RIBBED BUN HAT
Red Heart® Soft®
#9518 Teal

RIBBON BUN HAT
Red Heart® Soft®
#9114 Honey

WIDE HEADWRAP
Lion Brand® Vanna's Choice®
#173 Dusty Green

FLORAL HEADWRAP
Lion Brand® Vanna's Choice®
#135 Rust

WIDE BRIM BUN HAT
Red Heart® Unforgettable®
#3935 Dragonfly

SLOUCHY HAT
Premier Yarns® Deborah Norville Collection Everyday®
#200-03 Winding River

TWO-TONE BUN HAT
Premier Yarns® Deborah Norville Collection Everyday®
Pink - #100-32 Peony
Cream - #100-02 Cream

CABLED BRIM HAT
Red Heart® Soft®
#9820 Mid Blue

CLUSTER BUN HAT
Red Heart® Soft®
#9010 Charcoal

Production Team: Instructional/ Technical Editor - Sarah J. Green; Editorial Writer - Susan Frantz Wiles; Senior Graphic Artist - Lora Puls; Graphic Artist - Victoria Temple; Photo Stylist - Lori Wenger; and Photographer - Jason Masters.

Made In U.S.A.